SO WHAT DOES GOD SAY?

Healthy Thinking for Victorious Living

So What Does GOD Say?

So What Does GOD Say?

This book is a tool designed for those who are struggling with maintaining healthy thoughts during a time when life can become overwhelming with negative influences. The mind is a powerful tool that when exposed to the proper influences, can guide a person with such force they cannot be stopped.

Humans use 100 percent of their brain to function; contrary to the implied 10 percent most of us have heard from various sources. The brain is already performing at 100 percent and doing all it can, when it can. While some brains can process and maintain information better than others, the brain still functions at 100 percent unless afflicted with a disease or is fatigued.

So what does God say about our minds? *"Summing it all up, friends, I'd say you'll do best by filling your minds and meditating on things true, noble, reputable, authentic, compelling, gracious—the best, not the worst; the beautiful, not the ugly; things to praise, not things to curse. Put into practice what you learned from me, what you heard and saw and realized. Do that, and God, who makes everything work together, will work you into his most excellent harmonies. "* (Philippians 4:8-9 Message Bible) So there you have it; we have been commanded by God to think on the best things.

Thought power is the key to creating your reality. Everything you perceive in the physical world has first been birthed in the inner world of your thoughts and beliefs. The conditions and circumstances of your life are as a result of your collective thoughts. Pretty sobering. Truth is, your feelings are not a result of your present circumstances but a reflection of your thought power that is creating those very circumstances, whether wanted or unwanted.

It is your subconscious mind that is the storehouse of your deep-seated beliefs and thoughts. In order to change your present circumstances and attract to yourself that which you choose, you must learn to train and retrain your subconscious mind.

So what does God say? *"This book of the law shall not depart out of thy mouth; but thou shalt meditate therein day and night, that thou mayest observe to do according to all that is written therein: for then thou shalt make thy way prosperous, and then thou shalt have good success."* (Joshua 1:8 KJV) God commands us to center our thoughts on His Word knowing how powerful the brain is in controlling our actions. You are not a victim of your present condition, but a participant. The good news is, you can change your affiliation whenever you desire. Are you ready? Let's go!

Surrendering your current thought life is the first step toward many in building a healthy mindset. As we have already learned, how you think and view situations directly impacts your reality. My desire is to give you the tools to create a life giving subconscious that will push you into a productive and impactful life filled with Gods blessings.

Have you ever encountered a person who seems to not allow anything to bother them? When adversities come their way, on the outside it seems as though those situations just roll off their backs like water on a duck. Is this really the case, or could it be they understand that what they meditate on will form their present circumstances? I say, the latter of the two.

So what does God say? *"Consider it a sheer gift, friends, when tests and challenges come at you from all sides. You know that under pressure, your faith-life is forced into the open and shows its true colors. So don't try to get out of anything prematurely. Let it do its work so you become mature and well-developed, not deficient in any way."* (James 1:2-4 Message Bible)

So What Does GOD Say?

Well, there you have it. It is not that those people don't encounter adversities but their success comes in how they deal with the situation. The thoughts they meditate on concerning the issues are positive and uplifting in spite of how it looks on the outside. You too can direct your mind power in the same way and experience peace.

It is important for you to understand that your current thought patterns were formed as a child. How you dealt with disappointments, discipline, change, or losses can shed light on how you process those same situation currently. Each one of those experiences made an impression on the surface of your mind. The great news is with work, you can change those early impression into strong healthy ones that will allow you to walk daily in a positive light.

So what does God say? *"For we wrestle not against flesh and blood, but against principalities, against powers, against the rulers of the darkness of this world, against spiritual wickedness in high places.*" (Ephesians 6:12 KJV) So you see, this issue is foundational yet God tells us that *"The world is unprincipled. It's dog-eat-dog out there! The world doesn't fight fair. But we don't live or fight our battles that way—never have and never will. The tools of our trade aren't for marketing or manipulation, but they are for demolishing that entire massively corrupt culture. We use our powerful God-tools for smashing warped philosophies, tearing down barriers erected against the truth of God, fitting every loose thought and emotion and impulse into the structure of life shaped by Christ. Our tools are ready at hand for clearing the ground of every obstruction and building lives of obedience into maturity."* (2 Corinthians 10:3-6 Message Bible) Wow, if that doesn't make you stick your chest out!

Now the journey begins. Let's start by asking God for help in changing our thought patterns. Repeat this prayer:

> Father God, I know that every good and perfect
> thing comes from you. I know that you knew me
> before the foundations of the earth and that every
> hair on my head is numbered. I ask you today to
> cleanse my mind of all thoughts that are not pure.
> All thoughts that do not line up with your Word.
> Teach me how to meditate on those things that are
> peaceful and uplifting. In Jesus name, Amen.

You have officially brought God into the situation. Change
must occur; that's good news! Only the power of God is
strong enough to break those habits of mental strong holds
that cause you to carry wrong thinking around with you all
day. No wonder you are tired and stressed out. If it is a
situation you can change, then fix it. Otherwise, let it go
and focus on all the wonderful and positive things
surrounding you.

So What Does GOD Say?

So what does God say? *"The thief cometh not, but for to steal, and to kill, and to destroy: I am come that they might have life, and that they might have it more abundantly."* (John 10:10 KJV) There is no question that wrong thinking is not Gods will for your life. He has given us the tools to live a joyous and peaceful life; consistently. That's good news!

You must replace the negative thoughts with positive and truthful thoughts. God has already explained that He wants you to meditate on those things that are positive. This will not happen automatically just because you now want it to. You must undo this pattern, kill it at the very root. Be committed to continually killing the root until those patterns no longer control your mind.

So what does God say? *"Take your everyday, ordinary life—your sleeping, eating, going-to-work, and walking-around life—and place it before God as an offering.*

So What Does GOD Say?

Embracing what God does for you is the best thing you can do for him. Don't become so well-adjusted to your culture that you fit into it without even thinking. Instead, fix your attention on God. You'll be changed from the inside out. Readily recognize what he wants from you, and quickly respond to it. Unlike the culture around you, always dragging you down to its level of immaturity, God brings the best out of you, develops well-formed maturity in you." (Romans 12:2 Message Bible) The Word of God is strong, clear and applicable. Apply it to your life now.

Identifying those areas in your life that tend to generate negative thoughts and weigh heavy on your heart will help you know where to begin to pray. Prayer is simple talking to God. Share your thoughts whether positive or negative. Asking Him for guidance on how to process situations and circumstances that are affecting your emotions. You have a resource; use Him. I promise you He does not mind. Repeat this prayer:

So What Does GOD Say?

> Father God, I ask that you show me in the spirit of
> my mind every area in my life that causes me to
> think wrong thoughts. Any situation that allows me
> to remember painful memories. Show me any
> relationships that drive me to those negative places
> in my subconscious. Reveal habits that put me in
> an emotional state of feeling defeated. I ask this in
> your son Jesus Christ, Amen.

Get ready to receive your answer. Prepare to do some work
to change those areas He identifies. This may require you
to change your behavior in some parts of your life,
disconnect relationships with some people or even get rid
of some items that are holding you back with negative
memories. Remember, killing the unfruitful thoughts in
your mind at the root, is the only way to your victory. You
can do this!

So What Does GOD Say?

What are some of the things that the enemy is whispering in your ear? Yes, I said the enemy. Those negative thoughts that you hear are not from God. He loves you and only sees the person he created. And although we tend to believe that God judges us like man judges that simply is not true. You must grab hold to that truth and use it against the negative thoughts that cause you to disconnect from the love of God. Did you know that you can grieve the Holy Spirit with your thought life? Well, it's true. God never wants us to think about negative things. He desires that we pray and give those thoughts and concerns over to Him and trust that He will take care of them.

So what does God say? *"I beseech you therefore, brethren, by the mercies of God, that you present your bodies a living sacrifice, holy, acceptable unto God, which is your reasonable service."* (Romans 12: 1 KJV) This scripture includes your thoughts. Before we do anything as a human being, it first must appear as a thought in our mind. We then decide what to do with that thought. With every thought, God gives us the ability to choose what we are going to do with it. Your life will be healthier and more productive when you respond only to healthy and productive thinking.

No matter what mistakes you have made or what background you come from; God loves you with an unconditional love. Please take a few minutes and meditate on that. He desires you to live happy, healthy, free from worries and have the ability to do what you have been created, by Him, to do on this earth. When you are bogged down with negative thinking; you are not able to hear from Him and do things accordingly. That is the trick of the enemy. Don't let him win.

So what does God say? *"For I am convinced [and continue to be convinced—beyond any doubt] that neither death, nor life, nor angels, nor principalities, nor things*

present and threatening, nor things to come, nor
powers, [39] nor height, nor depth, nor any other created
thing, will be able to separate us from the [unlimited] love
of God, which is in Christ Jesus our Lord." (Romans 8:38-
39 AMP) That settles it. No more shall you waste any time
on wrong thinking. Hallelujah, you have the victory!

Let's seal this thing with prayer. Repeat after me:

> Lord Jesus, I thank you for the understanding of
> your love for me. I know that you love me and that
> you desire nothing but the best for me. I don't have
> to waste time believing the lies of the enemy. I
> commit today to meditating on the promises of
> Father God and building myself up in the love of
> Christ. I thank you in advance for the victory in my
> mind. In Jesus name, Amen.

So What Does GOD Say?

Now, I want to talk with you about your daily thought life. You have learned that negative thoughts come from the enemy. You have also learned that God desires you to meditate on healthy and joyous things that will build your faith in Him. You have prayed and asked God for victory in your mind. You know that you have the love of Christ on the inside of you and have been created to do great and mighty things in the earth. However, you must do your part each day to ensure that you will have great success.

Reverse the curse. Dealing with the root of those thoughts will take daily application of the Word until you know longer believe what your mind is telling you. Are you holding unforgiveness toward someone? You are probably replaying the situation over and over in your mind. When you focus your thoughts in this way, you never truly heal from the pain or disappointment that person caused. You must forgive so that you can let loose the hold that person or situation has over your mind. Are you still feeling pain from a broken relationship? It took a long time for me to understand that God places people in your life for a season. However long that season may be; even if they leave in a negative way it was ordained for them to leave.

So what does God say? *"To everything there is a season and a time for every purpose under heaven."* (Ecclesiastes 3:1 NKJV) It may not seem like it now, but this is the comfort that God provides in His Word. This is why it is so important to cherish the healthy relationships we have and not waste even one moment on unhealthy ones. Move past the pain of a divorce, a broken friendship, or an unproductive relationship. Know that God has provided a season of healing and restoration. But it first starts with your thoughts which will then fuel your actions.

As I mentioned in the beginning, this book is a tool designed to assist you with maintaining a healthy and productive thought life filled with positive and uplifting thoughts that will propel you into your purpose. But you will need to work daily to achieve victory in your mind. It has been said that if a person continues any activity for 21 days or longer it will become a habit. It will be like a second nature for them to continue that activity. In other words, it becomes part of their lifestyle and they would have to intentionally discontinue the activity for 21 days to remove it from their subconscious. Well, if this is the case then it is time to create your new thinking process. You are going to train your mind to think the way Gods Word tells us to think. And yes, it will take at least 21 days before your thoughts will heal and become positive and uplifting in the midst of adversity and despair. Now, that doesn't mean that you will never have a wrong thought. What it does mean is that it will be effortless for you to change that negative thought around into a positive and productive one that lines up with the Word of God.

The words on the following pages represent 21 days of positive, affirming, and uplifting statements that will train

So What Does GOD Say?

your mind to fight against unhealthy thoughts invoked by
internal or external situations. It is important to read these
statements out loud several times a day, each day and
reflect on how much God loves and values you as His
creation. This is a process and cannot be done half-
heartedly. However, I know that with faith and patience,
God will begin to change your outlook on life within your
mind. When you know better; you do better. Be Blessed.

Day 1

I choose to look at today through new eyes. I choose to see past my current situation and hope for tomorrow. I realize that I am in control of my destiny and today I make the choice to live happily in the moment. I was created for a purpose. And although I don't have all the pieces yet, I trust that God has a wonderful plan for my life full of opportunities, health, love, stability, security, and forgiveness. I forgive myself for any wrong decisions I may have made in my life knowingly and unknowingly. God is a God of grace and mercy and I allow myself to receive His grace and mercy concerning the choices I have made. I forgive anyone who has committed a wrong against me knowingly and unknowingly. I refuse to allow the pain and hurt from their actions continue to cloud my thinking. I am no longer a victim but choose today to take back the mental power that was held over me.

Day 2

I will to love again. My heart has been broken in the past, however, today I choose to tear down the walls I have built out of hurt and allow myself to love and be loved. God is the giver of love and He desires me to experience His kind of unconditional love. I will open my heart to receive as well as give this kind of love to another. Love gives; it is not selfish and it is not boastful. I celebrate the love God has allowed me to experience in my life and I embrace the love yet to come. My love for people extends past any wrong doing and I will make the choice to erase the memories of such, just as God does on my behalf each day I awaken. I meditate on the goodness in people and look beyond the flaws that sometimes overshadow them. I desire my presence to release peace and cause the light of Christ to shine brightly and warm the souls of those around me. Love really does conquer all and today I choose to be the conqueror of all my situations.

Day 3

I wear strength like a crown upon my head shining with rubies, diamonds, and delicately placed pearls. I live my life not in my own ability but the strength of Jesus Christ that is within me. I will not fear what I do not understand. But I will seek wisdom and knowledge so that I will be able to stand with strength through the storms of life. The race is not given to the swift; therefore I will not compromise my principles in the belief that I must make the first move. But I will rely on the safety of God and know that I am well able to endure through any obstacles until the very end. I am willing to stand, even if that means standing in what seems to be a lonely place in life. For I know that God is with me and through Him I can achieve and excel in every area of my life. I am a strong person, willing to embrace what life has in store for me knowing that I can accomplish all things through Christ who continuously gives me the strength I need to survive.

Day 4

When I look in the mirror I see the reflection of a person dawned with beauty which was given by the Father in heaven. I embrace my total outward appearance and I understand that it is only part of who I represent. The love I have on the inside of me makes up the other part. I am satisfied with my whole self. I choose to develop those areas that I feel would make me a better person. Not because the world says I need to but because I know it will help me live my life on a higher level. I am committed to living a healthy lifestyle full of good nutrition, exercise, proper rest, and meditation. Every inch of me was uniquely created with love and patience by God Himself. Even the hairs on my head are numbered and accounted for by God. Therefore, I refuse to allow negative thinking concerning my appearance to consume me. Nor will I condone any person speaking negative words concerning my appearance. I am made perfect in the sight of God and I except and embrace that fact. I love and cherish myself.

22

Day 5

Perfection is not something I strive for because there is no such thing. I strive to be the best person I can be. I do not compare my abilities to others as a way to define my accomplishments. I understand that I am an individual with my own set of skills, talents, and abilities. I celebrate each one of them and believe that they are my unique identifiers. I accept my mistakes and use them to learn about myself. I forgive myself quickly and accept the responsibility of admitting my part in any wrong doing. I refuse to hold grudges and will never attempt to manipulate a person or situation to achieve my goals. I will not subject my character to humiliation by conducting myself immorally. Apologizing when I am in the wrong does not make me a weak person but a human being. Transparency keeps me off the pedestal and humble before people. This is when my light can brightly shine toward the life of another.

Day 6

I refuse today or any other day to live in fear. I will not deny myself the pleasure of enjoying life because I am in fear of the unknown. I trust that Gods protection is constantly surrounding me. Fear is not a positive thought, but it is a negative emotion that will not dictate how I live day-to-day. Even if I am nervous, I will not let that stop me from stepping out in faith and trying something new. I am committed to life and I am committed to experiencing life to the fullest possible measure. I am a strong and confident person who can stand on my own two feet. Fear has no place in my mind or in my heart. When a fearful thought comes to mind, I will begin to speak only positive and affirming words over myself. I control my destiny as I continue to walk fearlessly through this tough world. I have the gifts and talents within myself to achieve any and everything I set my thoughts to. I seek wisdom, knowledge and support only from those who are willing to help me. Fear has no place in my life.

Day 7

Dreaming is not for the foolish. Dreams are ideas that come from my heart and are being planted in my core. Dreams are a healthy way for my mind to create pictures of how things could be in my life. I grow dreams and nurture them through my positive thoughts and actions. I will dream big dreams that seem impossible for me to achieve. As I begin to dream, God will show me ways to bring my dreams to life. Positive energy brings strength to dreams. Constant action brings growth to dreams. The emotion fear does not dwell with dreams. Fear is a dream stopper. I will not let the emotion fear hinder me from pursuing my dreams. I will write my dreams on paper, no matter how silly they may seem. I have the ability to turn my dreams into goals and those goals into reality. I will not procrastinate, but attempt each day to take a step toward developing my dreams. Positive energy brings positive results and dreaming is the spark that begins to move the positive energy. I commit to dreaming again.

Day 8

I don't just represent myself but I represent generations to come. Therefore, I understand that my actions today will create the results of my tomorrow. I desire to leave a legacy for the next generation of my family. I am not alone in this world but an intricate piece of the puzzle that makes up my family. My actions and behaviors matter. I matter. By seeking my purpose in life, developing and grooming myself, I will leave a mark of my existence on this earth. Legacy is not just for the rich and famous. I was created for a purpose and therefore I have a legacy inside of me that is intended to be passed on after I am gone. I will not live and die without using my gifts. I contain knowledge, love, wisdom, talent, and strength that will make an everlasting impression on this earth. The impact of my actions, words, giving, and creativity continue to fuel the next generation of my family. I have great influence over people and I choose to use my influence to do great things for my family, friends, and community. My legacy will inspire others to choose life, love, and hope in humanity.

Day 9

Today I walk in purpose, determined to fulfill all that I have been created to do. With the boldness that lies inside of me, I choose to exercise my gifts and talents to make a difference in my life, my family's life, and my community. Purpose is not earned but is assigned by God, tailor made to each individual. I will pursue and cultivate all skills and talents associated with my purpose so that I maximize my potential and impact in the earth. My purpose is unique to me and I will not compare my abilities to any other person. Nor will I apologize for any recognition or rewards of action I receive as a result of walking in my purpose. I am the only one who can fulfill the purpose God has given me and I trust and except whatever comes along with it. I will not be afraid of the hard work it will take to walk in my given purpose. But I realize that with any great responsibility comes sacrifice and dedication. Wonderful things are in store for me and I embrace them with a happy heart. I will guard my purpose by protecting my thoughts and actions against negative emotions.

Day 10

Determination is my daily motivation to walk through my life successfully. I will not look back over my shoulder wondering about yesterday, but I will keep my eyes forward and my feet moving toward the positive energy that flows from my heart. My determination creates a springboard that propels me into action and motivates me to stretch my faith and abilities even more then the day before. I understand that my footsteps are ordered by the power of God and I know I can trust that Gods path for my life is filled with everything I need to be successful. My part is to remain determined to seek that path and when it is found, stay on it no matter the storms of life that may blow. I am not weak but strong and well able to fight for the things that will improve my life. Defeat is not an option and I will not entertain negative thoughts of quitting, but will hold the rains of determination tightly until my hands become weak. Knowing that with time and patience every goal will become a reality in my life and will bring forth flourishing results. Strong determination is the key to my success.

Day 11

Gratitude is my attitude and I acknowledge all the wonderful things that are in my life. I am thankful for my family, health, and the provision that God has given me. Although I may not have obtained all that my heart desires, I am grateful for the progress that I have made so far. Holding on to past defeats will steal the opportunity for me to see the great and awesome blessings that I experience each and every day of my life. I take the time each day to reflect on God's grace and mercy and choose to celebrate His goodness. I wake each morning with great anticipation of what the day will bring. Each day I have the ability to open my eyes means I still have time to make an impact in the life of someone. I will consistently remind myself of all the precious gifts I receive on a daily basis. Gifts of love, friendship, health, provision, companionship, support, and trust from everyone who is in my circle of influence. I will not wait for perfection before I display a grateful attitude. I will make the choice no matter what my current situation is to focus my mind on thoughts of gratitude.

Day 12

Today is my day to take action. To put into motion those projects that have been in my thoughts for years. Today is the day I change those things in my life that I don't agree with anymore. Taking action requires me to move from where I currently am toward where I want to be. No one can take action on my behalf. Each step I take, whether big or small will eventually get me to my set place. I celebrate the small and the big steps alike. Taking action requires ongoing confidence that there are greater possibilities that I have yet to discover. I will not be afraid of the unknown, but will remind myself every day that my actions are helping to develop me as a better person. Procrastination is the enemy and I will not allow it to dominate my actions. When I feel overwhelmed with life, I will take the time to reach up for help from God and then I will keep moving forward. I refuse to allow moss to grow under my feet but I will flow with the currency of a river through life's obstacles. Confidence in who I am motivates me to take action and I will make my mark in the earth.

Day 13

Praying without stopping is what the Word of God commands me to do. Praying is just having a conversation with God. Just as I would with a friend or loved one. Praying creates a connection to my heavenly father that cannot be destroyed by anyone or anything. Prayer gives me strength in those areas where I am weak. Prayer allows me to release worries and concerns that plague my thoughts and cause me to doubt my abilities. I will not get so busy with the chores of life that I don't take time daily to have a conversation with God. He delights in spending quality time with me every day and looks forward to me sharing my heart with Him. I stand in confidence each day because I know that I have all of heaven protecting me and supporting me in all I do. Cultivating a daily prayer routine adds benefits to my life and causes my attitude to stay healthy and positive. Praying gives me hope in tomorrow because I know that God has already gone ahead to change those things that I need changed. I will take the time each day in prayer to thank God for all He has done for me.

Day 14

I desire to have healthy relationships. Relationships with positive and supportive people are a gift from God. I will not waste time on people who mean me no good. Healthy relationships allow me to develop as a person. In order for me to develop healthy relationships I must invest time in others. I must be vulnerable and not afraid to share my personal goals and thoughts with them. Some relationships may only be for a season in my life. Any relationship that I create must not take away from who I am, provide improper emotions, create pressure to lower my values or cause me to conduct myself in a manner that is embarrassing to me or my family. Jesus asked "how can two people walk together unless they agree on the same thing?" Therefore, I will not begin or develop a relationship with a person who I do not share the same values with. I will not hold on to any harmful or unproductive relationships. My time is precious and I will not waste it on foolish people. I am a good person and I make a great friend. I am thankful for all the relationships I currently have.

Day 15

My desire is to be trusted by God to handle the money I earn responsibly. This requires me to live within my means. I will not chase after another person's treasures but be content with what God has allowed me to receive. My resources are not only for my family but should be used to help others who are in need. A giving heart is a healthy heart. I am a liberal giver and take great joy in helping others. I will not be ashamed when God blesses me to receive financial increase. However, I understand that financial increase does not make me superior but it provides me more opportunities to be a vessel for God. I will be smart with my money and invest in my future and the future of my family by saving money in various ways. Wisdom does not allow me to spend all that I earn without storing something for tomorrow. I will teach my children the true purpose of money and train them on how to enjoy life and not be subject to material possessions. I will not create stress in my life because of poor money management but will seek assistance from an advisor when necessary.

Day 16

I walk in great power. I have the power to create change in the atmosphere. My existence is necessary to influence the people around me to become better and live out their full potential. Just my presence alone can create a spark that resonates in the earth. I have the power to change my situation and make it what I want. I am not at the mercy of my circumstances but I take full authority over them and strive to learn how to live a more purposeful life. I am not afraid of the journey, but will exercise the power I have on the inside of me to overcome any obstacles I experience. No one can take my inner power away from me. The feeling of helplessness is a negative emotion that is not real. God has given me everything I need to be successful. All I must do is tap into it through prayer and meditation on positive and healthy thoughts. Every mountain that I may encounter is a chance to determine my level of strength. I have the power to endure and to win in every situation in my life. I am strong and courageous.

Day 17

The joy of the Lord is truly my strength. Each day I will reflect on all the wonderful people that are in my life. Waking up with a sound mind that is strong and healthy is a blessing from God Himself. Each day I have the opportunity to find the joy in my life and give thanks. Having a thankful heart allows me to maintain joy and peace. Material things are not what provide lasting joy but love, family, and healthy relationships are what matter the most. A joyous spirit is contagious and can heal the broken hearted. I stand with a smile on my face and in my heart as I walk through life each day. Joy finds the sun in the mist of the clouds that may be looming over head. I use my joy to fuel my belief that my better days are ahead of me. I know that no one can stop my progress and I will take my journey through life full of joy and hope. Nothing can disqualify me from the love of God and I carry that joyous feeling with me every day. If my joy meter begins to register low, I will remind myself of the great life that I am experiencing. A joyous heart is a grateful heart and a grateful heart pleases God.

Day 18

Today is the first day of the rest of my life and I am excited about this day because God allowed me to wake up and breathe air. I have new opportunities today and I will seize the moment. I walk in happiness today, not because everything in my life is perfect. But I am grateful for my health, my family, and the resources God has entrusted me with. I have energy inside my body and my mind is sharp and clear. No more will I wake up and embrace the day in gloom and doom. I have a heart and mind of thanksgiving and I will walk through my day in peace. Tomorrow is not promised to me therefore, I will celebrate this day and will encourage myself. I am a winner in life and I will not waste time on feelings of defeat. Great opportunities are all around me and all I must do is walk in confidence and patience, and then I will receive the gifts and favor that await. There are great people assigned by God to help me with whatever I need. Therefore, I will not worry about what I don't have but I will focus on what I can do and trust God to make up the difference.

Day 19

How can I make a difference today? I know that I am not just living for myself, but I am living to help someone else. The more I give to others the more fulfilled I am. I will not continue to be a person who constantly takes and never gives anything in return. I am looking for opportunities to extend a helping hand, to uplift someone who cannot uplift themselves. I am seeking that next opportunity to reach out and support a fellow human being who doesn't have the courage to ask for help. I will allow my smile and happy heart to be a beacon, drawing those who are feeling hopeless. And although I am not equipped to save the world, I can love and encourage one person at a time. I am not afraid to stand in the gap for another person who needs support. I will never be too busy to listen with an attentive ear and an open heart. I will never be too busy to provide a shoulder to cry on or arms to hug. My greatest satisfaction in life is when I give of myself to another with no thought of the return. That is truly making a difference.

Day 20

I take no thought for how I am going to make it each day. I will not worry and doubt my abilities to take care of myself and my family. I can only control the present day, therefore I will not waste time wondering what will happen tomorrow. I can develop a healthy plan when I don't allow my thoughts to become negative and full of fear. I will view each situation calmly and without haste. I will seek counsel from people I trust when I don't feel I can handle the situation on my own. I have confidence that I will be successful in life with hard work and dedication to whatever I do. I will not be overtaken with the pressures of society by chasing things or status. I will not live above my means and cause unnecessary stress on myself or my family. I will conduct myself honestly and with integrity at all times because my name carries value and honor. Each day is full of possibilities for me and I will embrace each door that God opens on my behalf. I will enjoy each day with anticipation for what is next to come.

Day 21

I am refreshed and feel mentally stronger than I ever have in my life. This is a new beginning toward a more positive lifestyle. My old way of thinking and dealing with hard situations no longer exists. My new mind only focuses on the good things in life and is not afraid when difficult times occur. I know that God is with me and that I have everything I need on the inside to make it through tough decisions. I feel light as a feather in my heart and look forward to the better days ahead of me. I will surround myself with positive people who will help me grow in strength. When my heart feels heavy I will take time to pray and ask God for help. I refuse to carry negative emotional baggage. I will put all of my cares onto the shoulders of God and trust Him to deal with them. I will tap into the joy and peace inside of me to live victorious each day. Thank you God for this time of refreshing and healing of my mind.

So What Does GOD Say?

Scripture references from:

King James Version (KJV)
New King James Version (NKJV)
The Message Bible (Message Bible)
The Amplified Bible (AMP)

www.ingramcontent.com/pod-product-compliance
Lightning Source LLC
Chambersburg PA
CBHW060640030426
42337CB00018B/3404